D1806235

The Justin Jefferson Story

FOOTBALL & FAMILY

by Chad Israelson

illustrations
by Phil Juliano

LAKE 7 CREATIVE LLC

Minneapolis, Minnesota

To my sons, Addison and Garrison, and
to all young sports fans and book lovers.
—Chad

For Emmy, Luca, and Marlo.
—Phil

Acknowledgments: I express gratitude to my wife, Beth Butterfield, for her many suggestions, proofreading, and support. I would also like to thank Ryan Jacobson and Lake 7 Creative, LLC, for the opportunity to collaborate on this project. —Chad

Edited by Ryan Jacobson
Proofread by Emily Beaumont
Fact-checked by Chris Zobin

The information presented here is accurate to the best of our knowledge. However, the information is not guaranteed. It is solely the reader's responsibility to verify the information before relying upon it.

This book is not affiliated with, authorized, endorsed, or sponsored by the National Football League, its players, or anyone involved with the league. The use of any trademarks is for identification and reference purposes only and does not imply any association with the trademark holder.

JUSTIN JEFFERSON'S CAREER STATISTICS

COLLEGE

YEAR	TEAM	GAMES	RECEPTIONS	YARDS	AVERAGE	TOUCHDOWNS
2017	LSU Tigers	2	0	0	N/A	0
2018	LSU Tigers	13	54	875	16.2	6
2019	LSU Tigers	15	111	1,540	13.9	18
Totals		*30*	*165*	*2,415*	*14.3*	*24*

PROFESSIONAL

YEAR	TEAM	GAMES	RECEPTIONS	YARDS	AVERAGE	TOUCHDOWNS
2020	Minnesota Vikings	16	88	1,400	15.9	7
2021	Minnesota Vikings	17	108	1,616	15.0	10
2022	Minnesota Vikings	17	128	1,809	14.1	8
Totals		*50*	*324*	*4,825*	*14.9*	*25*

SUPERSTAR SPORTS BIOGRAPHIES

The Kirill Kaprizov Story
SMALL TOWN, BIG DREAMS
by Chad Israelson
artwork by Phil Juliano

The **Superstar Sports Biographies** aim to inspire children to read. Each picture book in the series presents the biography of a popular athlete from a professional sport such as baseball, basketball, football, or hockey. The biographies in this series are targeted to children ages 5 to 10 and are told as stories that are fun to read aloud. They include positive messages that promote character traits like integrity, kindness, and perseverance. Each children's book features full-color illustrations, includes the player's statistics, and is written by a sports fanatic.

"Go deep," Mr. John Jefferson said to his son Justin.

The boy ran straight down the field against his two older brothers, Jordan and Rickey.

The Jeffersons loved playing football together.

Mr. Jefferson launched a pass to Justin. The seven-year-old boy grabbed the football out of the air. Touchdown!

Justin's love of football continued to grow. Two years later, he showed off his skills in the NFL Pepsi Punt, Pass, and Kick competition.

Justin punted the ball, threw the ball, and kicked the ball farther than anyone else. The fourth-grader from Saint Rose Elementary School in Saint Rose, Louisiana, won first place in the state.

He wasn't finished yet. Justin entered the national contest on January 10, 2009. He won third place in the entire country!

Justin was not the only football star in his family. His older brother Jordan played quarterback for the Louisiana State University (LSU) Tigers.

Jordan played for LSU from 2008 to 2011. He passed for 4,733 yards and rushed for 1,018 yards. He helped his team post a record of 41–12.

Rickey also played for LSU. He was a defensive back from 2013 to 2016. He made 88 tackles and intercepted four passes in his career.

Justin loved to cheer on his brothers while they played.

Justin joined his high school football team in Destrehan, Louisiana. He became a star wide receiver for the Fighting Wildcats.

As a senior, Justin led his team to a 12–1 record in 2016. His Wildcats finished as the 11th best team in the whole state.

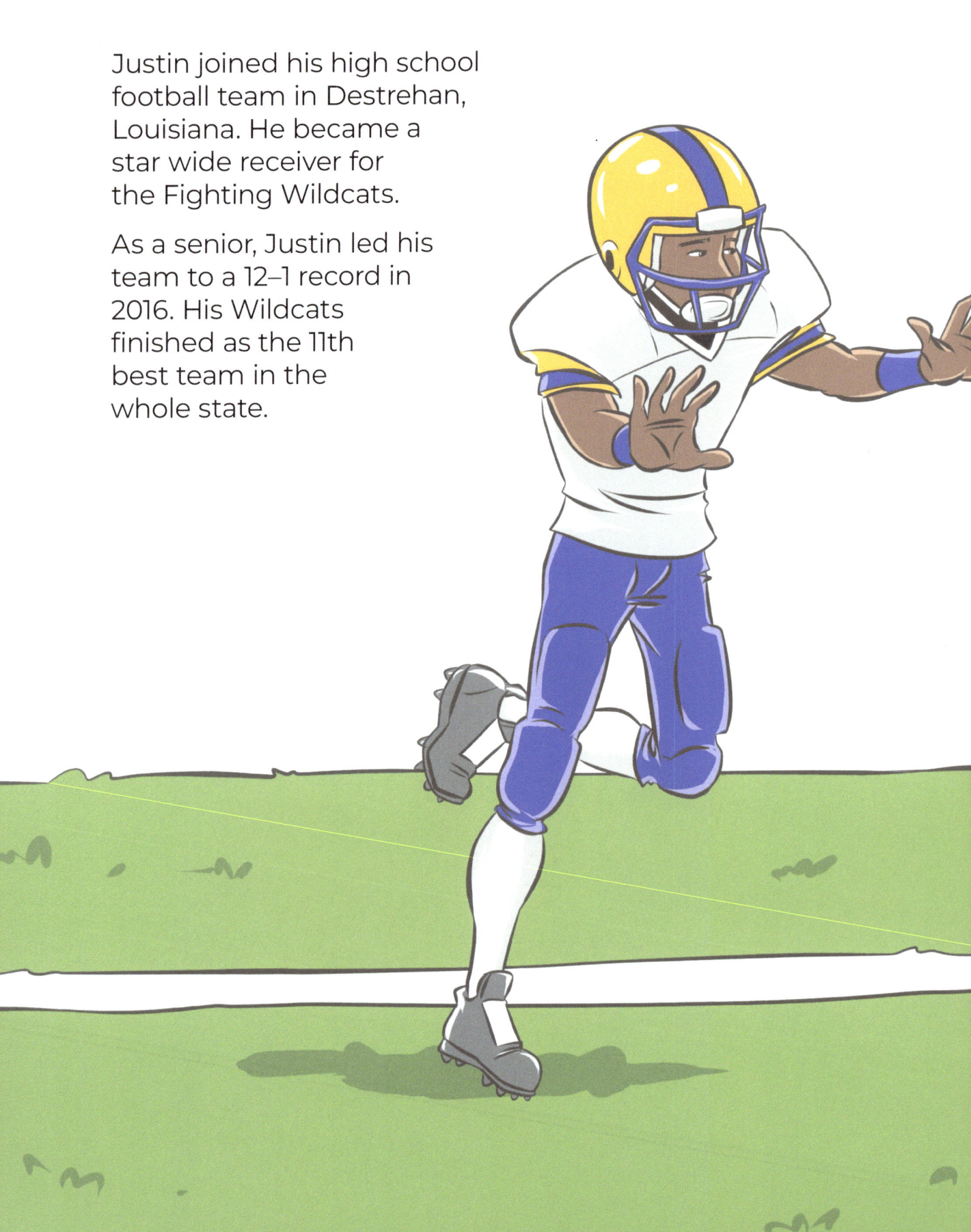

Justin did not rank among the best high school players in the country. Colleges didn't know how good he could be. Most did not recruit him to play for their team.

Justin graduated from high school in 2017. He decided to play football at LSU—the college his brothers had attended.

Justin did not play much during his freshman year of college. He did not catch any passes, and he ran the ball only once all season.

It was easy to feel discouraged. Justin's mom, Elaine, and the rest of his family said, "Don't give up."

Justin worked hard at getting better. A year later, he had a chance to prove what he could do.

Justin became the Tigers' leading receiver in 2018. He caught 54 passes for 875 yards, and he scored six touchdowns.

In his third season, Justin became a college superstar. He set LSU's all-time record for most receptions in a season with 111. He ended the year with 1,540 yards and 18 scores.

His team finished the regular season undefeated and went to the College Football Playoffs. In the Peach Bowl, Justin gained 227 yards receiving and scored four touchdowns. Both were Peach Bowl records.

Two weeks later, Justin's team played against Clemson for the national championship. LSU scored three touchdowns in the second quarter. They went on to win, 42–25. Justin caught nine passes for 106 yards in the game.

After his great season, Justin decided to leave LSU and enter the National Football League (NFL) draft. Justin waited with his family on April 23, 2020. They watched as four wide receivers were chosen ahead of him.

Finally, the Minnesota Vikings selected Justin with the 22nd overall pick. Justin and his family celebrated.

Justin's first two games in the NFL were quiet ones. He caught a combined five passes for 70 yards. In Week 3, he became a starter. He caught seven passes for 175 yards and scored his first NFL touchdown.

Justin went on to gain 1,400 yards. It was an NFL record for the most receiving yards in a season by a rookie. He was recognized as a top player in the league, getting chosen for the Pro Bowl. Justin was also named second-team All-Pro. Plus, he finished second in voting for NFL Rookie of the Year.

In 2021, Justin was even better. He caught 108 passes for 1,616 yards and 10 touchdowns. He was again a second-team All-Pro. Justin joined former greats Randy Moss and Sammy White as the only Vikings receivers ever to make the Pro Bowl in their first two years.

Despite Justin's success, the Vikings' record was just 15–18 with their star player. Justin would need to elevate his game even further to lift his team into the playoffs.

In 2022, Justin proved that he ranked among the NFL's best players. In Week 10, Minnesota trailed the Buffalo Bills, 27–23, in the game's final minutes. On fourth down with 18 yards to go, Justin made an amazing catch with one hand while falling to the ground. The 32-yard play gave his team a first down. Justin and the Vikings went on to win the game. The play was later named the NFL Moment of the Year.

In Week 14, Justin gained 223 receiving yards. That set a team record for the most ever in a game. Justin also set the team's single-season records for total receptions (128) and receiving yards (1,809). Those numbers were good enough to lead the NFL in 2022.

Justin was named first-team All-Pro, and he won the NFL's Offensive Player of the Year award. On top of that, his Vikings finished with a 13–4 record. They won the NFC North Division and made the playoffs.

In just three years, Justin rose to become one of the NFL's biggest stars. His touchdown dance "the Griddy" became so popular that Justin was the first NFL player added to the famous *Fortnite* video game. The game featured him dancing the Griddy.

Justin never forgot the people who helped to make his dreams come true: his family. With their support, Justin showed that a person can become great by focusing on goals and working hard to achieve them.

ABOUT THE CREATIVE TEAM

Chad Israelson grew up in Minnesota and began following the Minnesota Vikings at five years old. For the past 25 years, Chad has been a history instructor at Rochester Community and Technical College in southeast Minnesota, winning Outstanding Educator twice and serving as faculty president for six years. In addition, he taught history courses for Augsburg and Winona State universities. Chad serves as a political analyst for KTTC, Rochester's NBC-affiliated television station, and he was a columnist for Rochester's *Post-Bulletin*. Chad is an author of Minnesota sports books, including *Kings of the North*. He lives in Rochester with his wife. They have raised two sons.

Phil Juliano lives in Minnesota's Twin Cities, creating delightful illustrations for corporations, publishers, magazines, and more. He is a member of the National Cartoonists Society, and he is the creator of the syndicated comic strip *Best in Show*. When he is not drawing, he can usually be found outside somewhere, seeking his zen.

SOURCES

Schedules, statistics, and scores found at
• Pro Football Reference (pro-football-reference.com).
• Sports Reference: College Football (sports-reference.com).

"#2 Justin Jefferson." LSU Athletics (lsusports.net). Accessed September 2023.

Eckardt, Janik. "Justin Jefferson quietly broke 86-year-old record." Vikings Territory (vikingsterritory.com). January 11, 2023.

"Justin Jefferson." 247Sports (247sports.com). Accessed September 2023.

"Justin Jefferson places third in national contest." *St. Charles Herald Guide* (heraldguide.com). February 19, 2009.

MaxPreps (maxpreps.com).
• "Destrehan Football History." Accessed September 2023.
• "Justin Jefferson." Accessed September 2023.

Peters, Craig. "Justin Jefferson's catch named 'Moment of the Year' & Kirk Cousins sings with Kelly Clarkson." Minnesota Vikings (vikings.com). February 9, 2023.

Player, Gant. "The Peach Bowl's (other) star: Justin Jefferson." *Forbes* (forbes.com). December 31, 2020.

Smith, Eric, and Craig Peters. "Justin Jefferson goes back-to-back for Pro Bowl honors." Minnesota Vikings (vikings.com). December 20, 2021.

Milton Keynes UK
Ingram Content Group UK Ltd.
UKHW050213211123
432958UK00003B/87